A LIFE OF

ROBERT *B*URNS

J. D. Sutherland

illustrated by
Jane Dodds

APPLETREE PRESS

First published in 1997 by
The Appletree Press Ltd.
19-21 Alfred Street, Belfast BT2 8DL
Tel: + 44 1232 243074
Fax: + 44 1232 246756

A Life of Robert Burns
A catalogue record for this book is available from the British
Library.

ISBN 0 - 86281 - 643 - 2

9 8 7 6 5 4 3 2 1

ONTENTS

Volunteers firing a volley over Burns' grave

I

LAST DAYS OF A POET

ROBERT Burns was buried in Dumfries on 26th July, 1796, on the same day that his wife gave birth to their ninth child. He was thirty-seven and had died of a form of rheumatic fever whose cause and remedy were unknown at the time. In fact, Burns' 'treatment' had been the worst possible: he had been sent to undertake a course of sea-bathing and the immersions in chilly salt waters undoubtedly hastened his end.

The funeral was a ceremonious one. Burns had been a member of the Fencibles, the local volunteer force (Britain and France were at war), and his fellow-soldiers lined the streets between the Town Hall, where his coffin had lain on public view, and the churchyard of St. Michael's. 'Don't let the awkward squad fire over my grave,' the dying man had said, but three volleys were fired. In the moment of Robert Burns' death, the people of Dumfries, and very soon afterwards, the people of Scotland, realised they had lost someone incomparable. As is often the case, it was easier to recognise his worth after his death, than it had been when he lived. In life even a genius such as Burns had inconvenient moments, his share of human frailties and pressures. In death, only the genius and the works it has produced remains.

His fatal illness was not the result of a chosen lifestyle, but the direct consequence of prolonged and heavy physical work from a very young age, in a hard climate and on a very limited diet. It may not seem very poetic for a great poet to die of excess of work rather than of any of the excesses with which we are more familiar today, but Burns did not die of drink, he never suffered from venereal disease, and, apart from medicines, never took drugs. His illness was a physical one with no psychological dimension: it did not stimulate or affect his poetry - it merely cut it off in its prime. Today his condition would be diagnosed and cured almost as a matter of routine.

Burns' last days had been anguished ones. His wife was about to give birth again and he had a large family to support. He was in debt. His Volunteer's

uniform was not paid for and the tailor, whose business was dissolving, was pressing for payment. At that time even a small unpaid debt could lead to the humiliation of a debtors' prison. For a dying man, with many reasons for pride, the thought of such shame was intolerable. Burns borrowed the money owed: five pounds from George Thomson, the publisher of his collection of Scottish songs, *Select*

Scottish Airs, and ten pounds from his cousin, James Burness, in Montrose.

He had previously done a massive amount of work for Thomson without seeking any payment. There were two reasons for this: firstly, he would not,

or could not, put a price on his own work and, secondly, he regarded the job of gathering and preserving the riches of Scottish song as something far above the kind of daily activity that is justified only by payment. Thomson published the collection, many of its songs entirely written by Burns, most of the others revised, extended and built up by him from

8

fragments and variants. Like his predecessor, James Johnson, publisher of the Burns-compiled *The Scots Musical Museum*, Thomson was a prospector who had stumbled upon a gold mine which delivered its riches into his lap.

Yet despite the tightening grip of fatal illness, such was Burns' compulsion that he continued to write almost until the end. One of his most beautiful songs, *O Wert Thou in the Cauld Blast*, was written for a young girl, Jessie Lewars, who helped to nurse him at this time.

What kind of a man was this, who died poor and young, in a provincial town, and was almost immediately mourned by an entire nation? Other poets have been esteemed and loved, or have exemplified their country's soul and spirit, but Robert Burns is uniquely cherished.

ROBERT was William and Agnes Burnes' (they always spelt their name with an 'e') first child, arriving thirteen months after their marriage. The night of his birth, 25th January, 1759, was stormy and wild, as no doubt the parents told the little boy when he was older. Later he wrote:

There was a lad was born in Kyle,
But whatna day o'whatna style
I doubt it's hardly worth the while
To be sae nice wi' Robin.

Our monarch's hindmost year but ane
Was five and twenty days begun,

'Twas then a blast o' Janwar wind
Blew hansel in on Robin.

The place was Alloway, in the district of Kyle, in Ayrshire. His father had built the family house with his own hands. Constructed from clay and lime, it was a typical small Scots farmhouse with a stone doorway and chimney; inside, the living-room, kitchen, barn and byre were all housed under one long, low, thatched roof. The house is still preserved, though it is no longer set among fields.

The boy was baptised Robert, but was known to family and friends as Robin, and grew up in a home that was perhaps the best of its kind. His father was a somewhat austere man, deeply religious, and often preoccupied by the difficulties of a small tenant farmer struggling to make a living on poor soil. His mother was a woman of strong personality and fiery temper, a hard worker who sang as she worked, and the songs she sang were the traditional songs of the countryside and the popular ditties of the day. However, Robert never seemed to be particularly close to his mother, who was to long outlive him, and who preferred his more staid and settled younger brother, Gilbert. The parents did not have aspirations for themselves or their children, beyond the normal hope of the boys keeping the family farm and earning a sufficient living from it, and the girls marrying into other farmers' families. But that did not stop them from educating their offspring.

Robert and Gilbert first went to school at Alloway Mill, two miles away. But then Robert's father arranged for his children and those of three other families in the neighbourhood to share a private teacher. The teacher was paid sixpence a day plus board and lodging. The young man who took the post, John Murdoch, was only eighteen, and newly qualified. He taught the children English grammar, made them read and memorise chunks of the best literature, read the Bible with them, and made them sing the Psalms. Robert had not inherited his mother's gift of singing, and Murdoch is on record as saying Robert's voice was 'untuneable'. In the manner of the age, he encouraged the boy with a

leather tawse, but it made no difference.

The family then moved from Alloway to another farm at Mount Oliphant, two miles away and high on a hillside. When it was not Murdoch's turn to stay with them the boys walked down to Alloway and back for their lessons. The family owned few books, but borrowed books came and went, dire-sounding tomes like Hervey's *Meditations Among the Tombs* or *On Original Sin*. Much more to Robert's taste was *A Life of Hannibal*, which first introduced him to the 'romance' of military life.

Like all children, Robert learned as much from daily life as he did from tuition. And like all children, he learned best what appealed to his own taste and imagination. He picked up a lot from an elderly relative of his mother's, Betty Davidson, who helped about the place. Much of what he learned would have earned the disapproval of both his tutor and his father, for Betty had 'the largest collection in the country of tales and songs concerning devils, ghosts, fairies, brownies, witches, warlocks.' This store of knowledge would certainly have endeared Betty to

15

young Robin, who was an imaginative child. Indeed he was so impressionable that when John Murdoch read from Shakespeare's *Titus Andronicus* one evening, the violence in the play so horrified young Robert that he wanted to burn the book.

Life at Mount Oliphant was hard. Burns' father came to realise that he had made a bad bargain by renting this exposed and sour upland ground. He owed money to the landlord, and had not been able to sell the cottage at Alloway. Despite living on a farm, the children were fed only oatmeal and skimmed milk; meat was much too expensive. It was on this scant diet that the nine-year old Robert did a hard day's work in field and farmyard, for the family could afford no paid help. Through it all, William Burnes tried to instil a respect for learning in his children: he spoke seriously to his sons, and tried to lead them to discuss ideas, if mostly of a theological and moral sort. While at table, they were encouraged to read; sitting with their borrowed books, silent over the frugal meal.

In 1772, Murdoch became a master at Ayr Academy, and occasionally came to Mount Oliphant for a 'mental feast' with the family. In addition he offered free lessons to Robert, which released Robert from his tasks to go to Ayr for a week or two at a time. The lessons included tuition in French, the language of the new intellectual, political and emotional ideas which were spreading across Europe. Robert became increasingly aware of the riches to be found in books, and exploited every contact to borrow works of history, novels, poetry; even a Latin grammar. The light available in the long, grey Scottish dusk, was a single candle and Robert was usually to be found huddled beneath it. Gilbert noted later:

17

My brother... at fifteen was the principal labourer on the farm, for we had no hired servant, male or female. The anguish of mind we felt under these straits and difficulties was very great... I doubt not that the hard labour and sorrow of this period of his life, was in a great measure the cause of that depression of spirits with which Robert was often afflicted through his whole life afterwards.

When the landlord, who was a relatively benevolent figure, died, the factor who managed the estate became an authoritarian presence in the lives of the Burnes family. Robert was to write, describing the same period:

A Novel-writer might perhaps have viewed these scenes with some satisfaction, but so did not I: my indignation boils yet at the recollection of the scoundrel tyrant's insolent, threatening epistles which used to set us all in tears.

The heartless behaviour of the factor played its part in the development of the man who would one day send cannons to help the French revolutionaries.

But Robert was also bitterly aware of how neither his education and knowledge, nor his natural ability were going to liberate him from a lifetime's drudgery on the farm. Some of his school fellows would go on to university, the law or medicine, but these choices were not open to him. Despite his father's reverence for learning, there was no money to spare.

This kind of life, the cheerless gloom of a hermit with the unceasing moil of a galley-slave, brought me to my sixteenth year; a little before which period I first committed the sin of RHYME.

The isolation and the gloom were not total, however. When he was fifteen, he wrote his first love poems, to a farmer's daughter from Dalrymple, Nelly Kirkpatrick. Love and poetry were always to run together for Burns; and the boy who could not sing possessed a deep, instinctive and sure feeling for rhythm and tune. For Burns to write a love song, he first had to have the tune inside his head - but the tunes came with ease.

19

Tarbolton Village

III

THE DISCOVERY OF A BARD

IN 1777, when Robert was a handsome, dark-eyed young man of nineteen, the family moved again, to a farm at Lochlie, in a damp valley close to the village of Tarbolton. It was a lively place filled with cottage industries: weaving was carried on in many of the houses. Robert had discovered the novel *The Man of Feeling*, a work of now unreadable sentimentality which obsessed the nation at the time. Henry Mackenzie, its author, was seen as Scotland's senior man of letters. Robert tried out the mannerisms of the vapid hero of the tale, though, ironically, he himself was becoming a man of far more sensitive, true and well-expressed feeling. He made friends of both sexes among the local youth, and played a leading part in their flirtatious games and

assignations. He had become a skilful letter-writer
and penned many a love-note for less literate swains.
But flowery letters were not enough; he had an
overwhelming urge to make poetry. He wanted his
verses to be poetry that was meaningful to himself, his
family and friends; poetry that arose out of the rivers,
dales, fields and daily events of his own countryside,
not imitations of the florid verses he read in printed
books.

Following his natural desire for sociability, he
founded a debating society, the Tarbolton Bachelors,
with his brother Gilbert and a few others. The
Bachelors met in the upstairs room of a local tavern
each week and discussed such topics as "Is a savage
or a civilised peasant the happier?" The evening
ended with the drinking of ale and a toast to
sweethearts. Robert's chosen sweetheart was Alison
Begbie, a farmer's daughter who worked on a local
farm, but however forward he was on behalf of
others, he was slow to make a formal approach for
himself. He was earning only seven pounds a year
from his father; not nearly enough to set up on his

own. When he did eventually write a letter of proposal to Alison, she politely turned him down. Meanwhile, the family decided there might be more profit in growing flax, the staple of the linen trade, and Robert was sent to the coastal town of Irvine to learn the stages of flax-dressing. The Alloway house had at last been sold, and money was a little readier than before.

Burns at nineteen

Raking out the tow from the flax-plants in a dusty back-shed had no appeal to the young man. He fell ill, wondered if he would die, and wrote. On New Year's Eve, 1781, after a wild party at his shared lodgings, the place went on fire, and the few possessions he owned were destroyed. On a happier note, he discovered Templeton's bookshop, where he was introduced to the work of Robert Fergusson and found that he was not the first to conceive of writing verses about every-day life, in his own speech. However, Fergusson had died poor and mad, aged

23

only twenty-four: not the best of omens. He was already half-forgotten, but Burns took heart and inspiration from Fergusson's poems and cherished his memory.

Following the fire, Burns took rooms on his own and led his own life. Flax-farming had turned into a lost dream: his father was a sick man, prematurely aged, and now engaged in a hopeless legal dispute with their landlord. As a result, Robert returned to the family home. After Irvine he felt more assured about himself: there had always been a powerful will behind his shyness and now that will became more evident. If, Burns reasoned, he was condemned to be a ploughman in a country parish, at least he would show those around that he was no ordinary ploughman. Consequently he dressed for effect; everyone wrapped themselves in a plaid to keep out the cold, but his plaid was a special colour. And he was the only man in the parish who wore his hair tied-back. However his 'making poems' was not unusual; there were many others who made verses, even if they were clumsy doggerel. Later in life,

Burns looked back on this period and said:

Poesy was still a darling walk for my mind, but 'twas only the humour of the hour. I had usually half a dozen or more pieces on hand; I took up one or other as it suited the momentary tone of the mind, and dismissed it as bordering on fatigue. My Passions when once they were lighted up, raged like so many devils, till they got vent in rhyme; and then conning over my verses, like a spell, soothed all into quiet.

Early in 1784 the Burnes family moved to the farm of Mossgiel, not far from the town of Mauchline. Once again it was a poor bargain and despite much hard work on Robert's part, it never made a profit. But at least here the landlord was a more congenial type. Gavin Hamilton, factor to the Earl of Loudoun, was a man of liberal ideas who, introduced to Robert by his clerk John Richmond, immediately became Burns' friend.

When Robert's father was

Jean Armour

dying, in February 1784, he called for all his children to gather around him. 'There is only one of you all I am afraid for,' he said. They all knew whom he meant: Robert had acquired a reputation for showing off, for disputation, for unconventional thinking, and for paying too much attention to the lasses. It was Robert's soul, rather than his body, that his father feared for - Lizzie Paton, the farm servant, was pregnant by him. Robert wept at his father's words, but did not change his behaviour. He tried to give up poetry, but it would not give him up. Scraps of paper with lines and verses filled a drawer. He had to stand up in church and be publicly reprimanded as the father of Lizzie's baby, but he refused to marry her.

Two years later, in September 1786, Jean Armour bore him twins. He made an informal marriage contract with her, but her infuriated parents forbade the union. At this time, to use his own phrase, his passions were almost permanently 'lighted up': he was in a constant fever of poetry, whilst also labouring on the farm, consorting with the Tarbolton Bachelors, making secret assignations with Jean Armour, and planning to escape from it all by emigrating to Jamaica. The enforced break with Jean dismayed and enraged him, but he soon found solace with Mary Campbell, a Gaelic-speaking girl from Argyll - the 'Highland Mary' of some of his late poems. He made rash promises to Mary and she too became pregnant, but she died in October, probably in childbirth, leaving two more parents to curse his name.

Burns' life may have seemed to be perpetually in a state of exhausting turmoil, but out of that chaos emerged a stream of wonderful poetry. He spoke of his work modestly but he knew it was good. The poems came in great variety, from the despairing lines of *The Ruined Farmer* to the sprightly ones of *The Tarbolton Lasses* and the proud defiance, perhaps to Alison Begbie:

> *Thou'rt ay sae free informing me*
> *Thou hast nae mind to marry;*
> *I'll be as free informing thee,*
> *Nae time hae I to tarry.*

He had found his characteristic note, that deceptively easy, informal, conversational tone that can communicate every feeling from anger to the most delicate tenderness, in words that did not come from the classical dictionary but from everyday speech. In the maelstrom that his life had become, he determined to make something durable - a printed book to contain and preserve the poems that meant more to him than he had ever admitted.

His poems had been passed around locally in manuscript form. They had made people laugh and cry, and struck far more deeply into their thoughts and emotions than the homely efforts of other rural versifiers. When Burns set up a subscription list, in April 1786, it soon reached over a thousand orders, more than enough to finance the printing. The Kilmarnock edition, named after the town where it was printed, came out in July that year and soon afterwards he found himself famous. Scotland had discovered that she had a bard.

Edinburgh in the 1780s

IV

S C O T L A N D ' S   B A R D

EDINBURGH in the 1780's, though no longer a political capital, remained the centre of the law and the church, and was still the cultural heart of Scotland. When Edinburgh heard of the Ayrshire poet and his book, it wanted to meet him; and so he rode there on a borrowed horse. He was nearly thirty and his mood was excited and hopeful, but wary. Literary society in the city was based around the university, the courts and the church but, at that time, for all its pride and confidence, it had few figures of any literary distinction.

The rustic bard was everything they might have hoped for: physically handsome, articulate, modest and appreciative of their hospitality and praise. Burns had powerful charisma and was a man of considerable presence. Just as he had held the centre of the stage in Tarbolton, so too did he in Edinburgh. He may have been more self-effacing, but his personality and the passion of his words when he was caught by enthusiasm were intensely memorable. Professor Dugald Stewart, shrewder than most, who had already met Burns in Ayrshire, noted his success, but added:

If there had been a little more of gentleness and accommodation in his temper, he would, I think, have been still more interesting; but he had been accustomed to give law in the circle of his ordinary acquaintance, and his dread of anything approaching to meanness or servility, rendered his manner somewhat decided and hard.

Burns was conscious of his low social standing; he knew too he was seen as something of a freak, like the 'Learned Pig' on show in the Grassmarket, and he looked hard, and often in vain, for signs of real friendship and a meeting of minds from his new acquaintances. He listened politely to their advice on how to polish his verses, but mostly ignored it. He wrote some stilted poems in the approved manner, in Augustan English, to show that he could emulate the 'best models', and these were greatly admired in the drawing rooms of literary Edinburgh; but he also wrote the mocking *Address to a Haggis*, which derides the pretensions he found in polite society. He also

sought out the neglected grave of Robert Fergusson in the Canongate cemetery and had a memorial stone erected to the unlucky earlier poet.

Caught between economic necessity and his acceptance into the wealthy homes of those who had

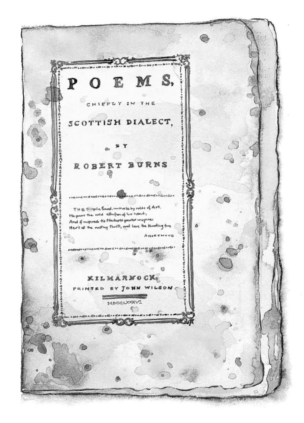

Title Page of the Kilmarnock edition

never known toil and hardship, Burns was under heavy strain. There was relief to be found in a drinking club, the 'Crochallan Fencibles', where printers' clerks and young lawyers, such as his friend Richmond who had moved to Edinburgh, gathered. At these convivial meetings in cellar taverns, his gift for instant epigrams and his enjoyment of bawdy verses would be shared and relished. He also had a romance with a working girl, May Cameron, and fathered another child. At the same time, he yearned to unburden himself to someone who would understand and sympathise with the opposing pulls and dimensions of his life. Mrs Dunlop, a well-to-do Ayrshire widow who admired his poems, seemed to fill this role, and she and he exchanged many letters, in which he told her his news with great frankness, and she responded with scoldings, advice and worthy admonitions.

In Edinburgh, a second edition of the poems was set in motion, this time with a publisher, William Creech. Sponsored by the new friends, the text was published in April 1787 and contained twenty-two

additional poems to the Kilmarnock edition. Editions
in London, Dublin, New York and Philadelphia soon
appeared but Burns made nothing from these.
Creech owned his copyrights, and the Irish and
American editions were pirated. Burns had hoped
that the visit to Edinburgh would result in his
receiving some kind of official position - one of those
common at the time, paying a respectable salary and
requiring little activity. But this needed sponsorship,
and Burns' admirers had unfortunately fallen for the
notion of the 'ploughman poet'. They envisioned him
back on the land, doing a little light agriculture and
throwing off poems as easily as he might brush the
sweat from his brow. He hoped for a modest position
in the Excise service, but even this seemed to be
hopelessly elusive.

Leaving Edinburgh, he set off to travel in the
Borders in order to see more of his own country. At
Selkirk on a rainy Sunday there was a revealing
moment. Burns and his companion arrived at an inn,
but the local doctor and his cronies, sitting by the fire,
refused to let the strangers have access to the warmth.

Only when Burns was gone did the doctor - a passionate admirer of the poems - discover, in dismay,

whom he had rejected. Burns' pride was fierce, but his early years had instilled in him a deference to his superiors. He did not have the social confidence to push in - even on the village doctor.

By summer 1788 he was back at Mossgiel farm, unsettled and still considering a new start in Jamaica. While at home he took up again with Jean Armour, and she bore him a second set of twins, who died. He also travelled through Argyll, staying at the houses of the gentry, writing poems of thanks and tribute. Then with an Edinburgh friend, William

37

Nicol, he went on an extended journey through the Highlands, as far north as Inverness. Wherever he went, he sought out the songs of the place, their words and melodies. Music and rhythm had always been inseparable from his poetry, but now the emphasis of his interest was shifting, from poetry to song. Rural Scotland was a treasure-house of local song, but a neglected one, with much already half-forgotten or corrupted. Burns not only collected these fragments, but breathed new life into them. During this restless season he proposed marriage to Peggy Chalmers, the clever and witty daughter of a gentleman-farmer. She refused him, but they remained friends.

On his stays in Edinburgh, he continued to have physical affairs with girls from his own class - Jenny Clow bore him a son in 1788 - while mingling with the literati. Somewhere between these two worlds was his relationship with 'Clarinda', Mrs Nancy McLehose, a lady who

Clarinda

lived separately from her husband. To her he was 'Sylvander', and they exchanged letters of often torrid emotion, couched in flowery language. Most of the poems inspired by Clarinda seem artificial compared to those he was writing at the same time to Jean Armour, as anyone may see who compares *Clarinda, Mistress of My Soul* with *Of A' The Airts the Wind Can Blaw*. When he eventually married the patient, humble Jean in 1788, Mrs McLehose dropped him with more than a touch of aristocratic revulsion. But as he had only recently written to tell her how much Jean disgusted him, perhaps he only had himself to blame. There was a short exchange of letters later with Clarinda, which resulted in the beautiful parting song, *Ae Fond Kiss*.

Burns' home at Dumfries

V

THE DE'IL'S AWA' WI' TH' EXCISEMAN

THE marriage to Jean coincided with a move from Mossgiel to another farm - Ellisland, near Dumfries. It had been pressed on him by a powerful friend, Patrick Miller of Dalswinton, banker, ironmaster and patron of inventors - but still there was a rent to pay, and Burns was very reluctant to continue the life of a farmer. He knew its drudgery and anxiety far better than his patrons and literary friends, who still saw his farming life as his inspiration, a rustic idyll which they were loath to deprive him of. And if Burns had to be a farmer, then in Jean he had the perfect farmer's wife; and she loved him sincerely and without jealousy or ambition.

Burns the farmer and Burns the poet were two

separate personas; he managed the affairs of one and retreated from them to pursue the destiny of the other. Scribes from all over Scotland, 'a shoal of ill-spawned monsters', sent him their efforts for his perusal. He was writing newspaper articles for a London paper, *The Star*, in which he aired his highly radical views, and for which he would accept no payment; and he wanted to write plays for the Dumfries theatre. Meanwhile he had, at last, been placed on a list of those suitable, after training, for an Excise post. However, Burns the revolutionary and Burns the government servant were to find it hard to exist together. He had admired the American struggle for democracy and had written an ode to George Washington, saluting him, 'Ye know, and dare maintain, the Royalty of Man!' When in July 1789, news of the French Revolution spread, he was one of those who welcomed it as a new dawn in human affairs.

In August he officially became an officer of the Excise, responsible for ensuring that the government got its tax on spirits, tobacco and other dutiable goods in ten parishes. There was never a customs officer like Burns; and it was for an Excise dinner that he composed and recited the galloping rant of *The De'il's awa' wi' th' Exciseman*, to vast appreciation and applause. The post was no sinecure: Burns had to cover nearly one thousand miles each month and sometimes the work was dangerous. At the head of an armed band he boarded a smugglers' vessel early

in 1792, and when everything on board was later put up for sale, he bought her cannons for £3 and had them despatched to the French government, at that time still identified with the cause of the 'rights of man'.

43

He had found a new friend and confidante,
younger, more intellectual and more vivacious than
Clarinda, in Maria Riddell, wife of a local landowner.
It was a platonic friendship and Maria, aged only
nineteen, was unconventional enough to visit the
Burns family at home. Burns' relationship with Anna
Park, a Dumfries barmaid, was rather more
passionate and the tolerant Jean took in the resulting
child. 'Our Rab should have had two wives' was her
only comment. Soon after there was a falling-out with
the Riddells after a drunken prank when the men
pretended to carry out a 'rape of the Sabine women'
on the womenfolk of the family. Burns' part in the jest
was no greater than anyone else's but, because he was
not a gentleman, he was felt to have crossed the
bounds of propriety in a way that was unacceptable.
He apologised profusely but was not readmitted to
Maria's circle. He salvaged his pride with some
wicked verses on the Riddells, but from then on was
more wary of the company of 'Honourables and
Right Honourables'.

He had to endure further humiliation for his

political views. Britain was preparing for war with revolutionary France and those who proclaimed support for France - let alone sent her armaments - were suspect characters. Burns had never made any secret of his anti-war views and general political radicalism, but when at the end of 1792, his superiors in the Excise set up an inquiry into his political conduct, he panicked. There was no quarrel with his official work, but the government of Scotland at that time was a Tory despotism, managed by the Secretary of State, Henry Dundas, and supported by men who owed their power to his patronage. Only a handful of people were eligible to vote, and their votes were bought: universal suffrage was still a dream. Minor government servants were not supposed to write for reformist and pacifist newspapers as Burns did. Even though a small but determined minority of his fellow-countrymen still spoke out in public for reform, and would have welcomed his continued support, he gave in, apologising for any improper behaviour and promising to be reliable in future. He was admonished by the inquiry; but it left him feeling doubly tarnished. Not only had he turned his back on his principles; but he believed that he had now lost all chance of promotion to a less arduous role in the Excise. In a bitter mood, he wrote:

> *In politics if thou would'st mix,*
> *And mean thy fortunes be;*
> *Bear this in mind: be deaf and blind,*
> *Let great folks hear and see.*

A few years before, as if foreseeing what might happen, he had written in *The Epistle to Dr Blacklock*:

> *I hae a wife and twa wee laddies;*
> *They maun hae brose and brats o' duddies:*
> *Ye ken yoursel's my heart right proud is -*
> *I need na vaunt -*
> *But I'll sned besoms, thraw saugh woodies,*
> *Before they want.*

In fact, by abasing himself to protect his livelihood, he did something much more painful to

Tam O'Shanter escaping from Cutty Sark

himself than make the brooms and willow-baskets mentioned in his verse. Bankruptcy, destitution, beggary, all seemed dangerously near to Burns throughout most of his life, and, partly through his father's teaching, partly through his own sense of achievement, he had a horror of crossing the narrow divide between poverty and penury.

The family moved to Dumfries town in 1791, when Burns finally gave up the life of a farmer, and they were packed into a cramped dwelling in a narrow lane, the Wee Vennel. The town was a bustling place, a centre of political, commercial and military life, with noisy taverns and a sprinkling of radical thinkers, whose company Burns enjoyed, as they did his. The family later moved to Mill Street, now Burns Street, where the house in which he was to die, like the house in which he was born, is kept as a museum.

Throughout this period, he was always busy collecting, refurbishing and writing songs, first for *The Scots Musical Museum*; later for Thomson's *Select Scottish Airs*. Burns' poetic energy was closely focused on this activity; it was literally a labour of love, for he refused to accept payment, and his publishers certainly did not force it on him. He saw the work as a mission beyond price, a national duty which only he was capable of doing in the right spirit. It was also at this time he wrote, on the request of his friend Captain Grose for a 'witch story', the splendid narrative poem *Tam O'Shanter*; an indication of what else he might have done, if the songs had not become such an obsession. The songs were his first passion, and, whatever else was happening, he never stopped work on them. There are two great strands in Burns' work: the satirical, political and narrative poems and the verse 'epistles'; and the songs which come in a wonderful variety and range, from Jacobite yearning to broad comedy, from tender love lyrics and beautifully detailed songs of place to the ribald and bawdy collection known as *The Merry Muses of Caledonia*.

Burns' life was a stressful one, that bore heavily on a physique weakened by the too-hard labouring of his childhood. As a result his bouts of illness and depression grew more frequent. When the war took hold and the French government became as indifferent to the rights of man as most others at the time, his enthusiasm for France cooled. He joined the Volunteers, as did many others of his views, perhaps glad to be able to show their essential patriotism, and ordered his uniform from the tailor. His family was large and growing - Jean became pregnant again late that year. Burns found himself hard-pressed for money: a generous lender to others, he found them slow and reluctant to repay. As his health sank, his worries about the future of those who depended on him mounted. On a few occasions in his life he had thought of death as a release; he had often written poems that proclaimed his own ability to face adversity; but now he feared its coming. So many depended on him and he still had so much to do.

VI

THE CONSTANCY OF THE HEART

BURNS the poet has never been out of fashion, though at different times and in different places he has been chosen to represent different things. His ardent Scottish patriotism has been of use to the nationalist cause; his political radicalism and championship of the working man made him the laureate of international Socialism; and his half-whimsical support for the lost cause of the Jacobites endeared him to traditionalists. In the twentieth century, his bawdy poems were taken to show that Burns was ahead of his own times as a writer whose range commanded the whole experience of love and sexuality.

Burns was a problem for the nineteenth century: the public facade that Victorian Scotland liked to present was decorous, devout and industrious. But Burns' Scotland of barnyard courtings and couplings, of religious hypocrites, of unscrupulous political fixers, of disreputable tavern wit, of a lingering half-belief in ghouls and ghosts was too recent and too real. His personal life: his out-of-wedlock children, his participation in drinking bouts, his cheerful contempt for the 'unco guid' could have been borne and set quietly aside, except that they were the stuff of his poetry. One of his earliest poems was *The Poet's Welcome to his Bastart Wean*. He was regarded as a somewhat dissolute figure, and it was commonly supposed that drink and sexual promiscuity had caused, or at least hurried on, his early death. The image of a reckless, idle, drunken poet was as false as the vision of Burns as a sensitive, gentle lover of nature, watching the little rivers flow among their green braes and penning a few charming lines.

In truth Burns was a man of great energy,

strongly-spoken, a vigorous presence in a room or a group. People who knew him said that his conversation and personality were even more memorable than his poems. He was always sociable and had a gift for friendship; he never cut himself off from his earliest friends and was all the more hurt by those, like Maria Riddell, who made their friendship conditional on his good behaviour. Many who have written about him have wished that they could

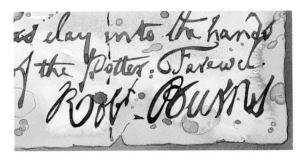

change the terms of his life: give him more stimulating and understanding literary friends; arrange for the well-paid official post with few duties; alleviate the terrible, drudging toil of his boyhood; marry him to the clever, sprightly Peggy rather than the dull, reliable Jean; and erase that shameful moment when to preserve his job, he renounced his most dearly held principles.

Despite his fame, he left no school of poets behind. His genius rose far above the offerings of contemporary rustic writers like his friend Davie Sillars, whom he generously saluted as a 'brother-

For a' that, and a' that,

That Man to Man, the world o'er,

poet'. No other talent of sufficient stature to maintain a Burns tradition came to light, either during or after his life. The lowland Scots he wrote was already a dying language: when the Kilmarnock edition was published, none of its subscribers needed a glossary;

but when the huge popular editions of the nineteenth century were printed, many of Burns' everyday words had to be explained. Lowland Scots had to be recreated in the twentieth century as a language of poetry. And the Scotland which Burns lived in and described, a land of tenant-farmers and cottage industries, was on the brink of drastic change, as large scale industrialisation began to spread. The winding gear of coal pits was shortly to adorn the green braes of Ayrshire. In 1786 in *The Address of Beelzebub*, he had attacked Highland landlords who would not let their tenants leave; soon they were forcing the tenants out.

A poet of the next generation, Lord Byron, said of Burns:

> *What an antithetical mind! - tenderness, roughness - delicacy, coarseness - sentiment, sensuality - soaring and grovelling, dirt and deity - all mixed up in that one compound of 'inspired clay.'*

But no genius is without contradictions. Even people of genius can have moral flaws; they are the

57

Burns' Monument and Gardens, Alloway.

product of their time, and though Burns in many ways transcended the Scotland of his day and in other ways reacted strongly against it, he also reflected it. In any case, to dwell too much on the contrary aspects of Burns is to ignore the essence of the poet: the spirit that drove him on through poverty, illness, depression, rebuffs, insulting patronage and constant hard work. He had a constancy of the heart in everything he did: his impulses were humane, generous, and high-minded. His tenderness was easily aroused - by a mountain daisy, a wounded hare or the teasing smile of a pretty girl - but in his best poems that tenderness is never mawkish, always controlled by his mastery of thought, rhythm and language. If tenderness and pathos are hallmarks of Burns, so too are racy humour and shrewd, vivid observation. People came before ideas for Burns. He had no faith in Divine Providence. The thought of his children going hungry was far more unbearable to him than grovelling to his official superiors. That constancy, and openness, of heart, so clear in everything he wrote, was what endeared him to his

59

fellow-countrymen, then and ever since.

Far beyond Scotland, his poetry has been seized upon by people to whom it speaks on international terms; his poems have been translated into more than thirty languages. He was, and is, identified with the still unachieved aspiration of the brotherhood of man, and the words written by him still have the power to make us feel we are, or can be, more than we allow ourselves to be:

> *For a' that, and a' that,*
> *It's comin' yet for a' that,*
> *That Man to Man, the world o'er,*
> *Shall brothers be for a' that.*